Math Masters

Operations and Algebraic Thinking

NOCTURNAL ANIMALS

Represent and Solve Problems Involving Multiplication

Jodi Lockerd

NEW YORK

Published in 2015 by The Rosen Publishing Group, Inc.
29 East 21st Street, New York, NY 10010

Book Design: Katelyn Londino

Photo Credits: Cover Ian Tragen/Thinkstock.com; pp. 3–24 (background) Tom Reichner/Shutterstock.com; p. 5 davewright321/Shutterstock.com; p. 7 Zoonar RF/Thinkstock.com; p. 9 HERGON/Shutterstock.com; p. 11 BMJ/Shutterstock.com; p. 13 (bats) tanaphongpict/Shutterstock.com; p. 15 Ivan Kuzmin/Shutterstock.com; p. 17 (main) HTU/Shutterstock.com; p. 17 (inset) Brandon Alms/Shutterstock.com; p. 19 Thomas Marent/ Visuals Unlimited, Inc./Getty Images; p. 21 Sascha Burkard/Shutterstock.com; p. 22 (lion) Jason Prince/Shutterstock.com.

Library of Congress Cataloging-in-Publication Data

Lockerd, Jodi, author.
 Nocturnal animals: represent and solve problems involving multiplication / Jodi Lockerd.
     pages cm. — (Math masters. Operations and algebraic thinking)
 Includes index.

ISBN 978-1-4777-4968-5 (pbk.)
ISBN 978-1-4777-4969-2 (6-pack)
ISBN 978-1-4777-6447-3 (library binding)

1. Multiplication—Juvenile literature. 2. Nocturnal animals—Juvenile literature. I. Title.
 QA115.L7 2015
 513.2'13—dc23
                                    2014000220

Manufactured in the United States of America

CPSIA Compliance Information: Batch #WS15RC: For further information contact Rosen Publishing, New York, New York at 1-800-237-9932.

CONTENTS

Animals at Night

What is a regular day like for you? You probably get up in the morning and go to bed at night. You may think nighttime is quiet and calm, but guess what? A lot of activity takes place while you're sleeping!

Our world is full of animals that are awake at night. Many critters sleep all day. When nighttime comes, they wake up and become active. These animals are called nocturnal. Read on to find out more about them.

Nocturnal animals live all over the world, including your own backyard.

Nocturnal animals have special **adaptations** that help them survive in the dark. Many animals have special eyes that help them see at night. Other animals have good hearing or a good sense of smell.

Animals are nocturnal for many reasons. Some animals are nocturnal because they can only find food at night. Other animals are nocturnal because it keeps them safe from danger. This includes avoiding high **temperatures** or predators that are awake during the day.

Desert animals are nocturnal because it helps them avoid the heat during the day. It's much cooler at night.

Hoot, Hoot

Have you ever heard an animal hooting at night? It may be an owl. Owls have many adaptations that help them hunt, including excellent eyesight. It's so good that they can see a mouse moving in the grass from a branch high up in a tree!

Imagine that an owl sits in a tree and waits to find food. If it dives 6 times and catches 1 mouse each time, how many mice does the owl catch?

This owl hunted 6 times, and it caught 1 mouse each time. It caught 6 mice, since 6 times 1 is 6.

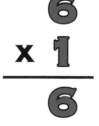

$$\begin{array}{r} 6 \\ \times\ 1 \\ \hline 6 \end{array}$$

Besides good eyesight, owls have a great sense of hearing. They're also very, very quiet. That's because their feathers make almost no noise when they fly. That's how owls sneak up on their **prey**.

Owls live where they can find the most food. They eat mice and other small animals, such as rats. Imagine that 3 groups of rats live near an owl's nest. Each group has 4 rats in it. How many rats live near the owl?

You can use multiplication to solve this problem. Multiply the number of rats in each group by the number of groups. Since 4 times 3 is 12, the owl lives near 12 rats.

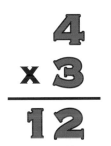

$$\begin{array}{r} 4 \\ \times\ 3 \\ \hline 12 \end{array}$$

Bat Attack!

There's another nocturnal animal that's also known for flying. It's the bat! Most bats are nocturnal because they eat bugs that only come out at night. What do bats do during the day? They sleep.

Bats hang upside down while they sleep. These bats are arranged in an **array**. To find out how many bats there are, multiply the number of rows by the number of bats in each.

In this array, there are 4 rows of bats with 5 bats in each. The array 4 x 5 is equal to 20, so there are 20 sleeping bats.

$$\begin{array}{r} 4 \\ \times\ 5 \\ \hline 20 \end{array}$$

13

Bats wake up when night falls. Then, it's time to hunt! Bats live in caves and other dark places. Sometimes, many bats will exit their home at the same time.

Imagine there are 60 bats in a cave. They leave the cave in groups of 10. How many groups of bats are there? Think of the number that makes 60 when you multiply it 10 times. It's 6, or 6 groups of 10 bats.

Equal groups can be placed in an array. By turning 60 into equal groups of 10, we can see that 60 bats makes 6 equal groups of 10.

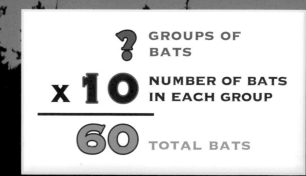

? GROUPS OF BATS

x 10 NUMBER OF BATS IN EACH GROUP

60 TOTAL BATS

GLOWING FIREFLIES

Many nocturnal animals hunt bugs, which means that some bugs are nocturnal. Have you ever seen tiny lights flying around the trees in your backyard? If you have, you've seen lightning bugs, or fireflies.

Fireflies live in groups. If there are 8 trees in a backyard, and they each have 9 fireflies flying around them, how many fireflies are there total? To find out, multiply 8 times 9. The answer is 72.

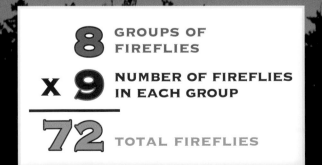

8 GROUPS OF FIREFLIES

x 9 NUMBER OF FIREFLIES IN EACH GROUP

72 TOTAL FIREFLIES

What if we know there are 72 fireflies, with an equal number around each of the 8 trees? That means there are still 9 in each group.

8 GROUPS OF FIREFLIES

x ? NUMBER OF FIREFLIES IN EACH GROUP

72 TOTAL FIREFLIES

Jungle Animals

You can find owls, bats, and fireflies in your own backyard, but some nocturnal animals live far away in jungles. One nocturnal jungle animal is known for its huge, glowing eyes. It's the slow loris!

The slow loris is an excellent climber. It climbs from tree to tree looking for food. If a slow loris climbs 8 tree branches that are each 5 feet long, how many feet does it climb altogether?

The slow loris climbs 40 feet total. Multiplying 5 feet 8 times makes 40 feet.

$$\begin{array}{r} 8 \\ \times\ 5 \\ \hline 40 \end{array}$$

The red-eyed tree frog is another nocturnal animal that lives in the jungle. It has bright red eyes and a bright green body. It doesn't move at all when the sun is out. Its green skin blends in with leaves during the day, which helps the frog hide from predators.

A red-eyed tree frog climbs more than it jumps. Imagine that a frog climbs 2 branches of equal length for a total of 36 inches. How long is each branch?

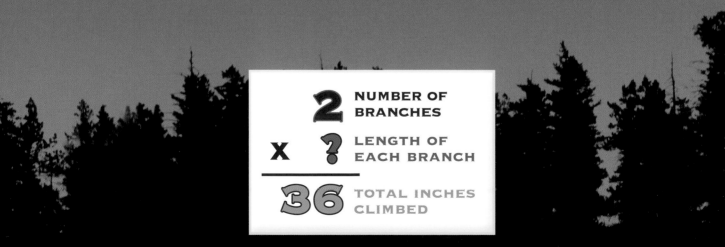

2 NUMBER OF BRANCHES

x ? LENGTH OF EACH BRANCH

36 TOTAL INCHES CLIMBED

To find this answer, think about what number makes 36 when it's multiplied twice. The answer is 18, because 2 x 18 = 36.

$$\begin{array}{r} 2 \\ \times\ 18 \\ \hline 36 \end{array}$$

2 NUMBER OF BRANCHES

x18 LENGTH OF EACH BRANCH

36 TOTAL INCHES CLIMBED

Time for Bed

Once the sun comes up, it's time for nocturnal animals to go to bed. Their bedtime occurs just as you're waking up! They'll sleep all day. Some animals blend in with their surroundings to hide and sleep. Others will go back to their nests or **burrows** to sleep.

When nighttime comes again, the nocturnal animals will wake up and start their day all over again!

GLOSSARY

adaptation (aa-dap-TAY-shun) A change in a living thing that helps it live better in its habitat.

array (uh-RAY) An arrangement of something in rows and columns.

burrow (BUHR-oh) A hole in the ground where an animal lives or hides.

prey (PRAY) An animal that is hunted by another animal for food.

temperature (TEHM-puhr-chuhr) How hot or cold something is.

INDEX